BEYOND IDENTITY POLITICS

The BIGGEST Mistake America Will Make: The Truth About Kamala Harris

Zoe Quinn

Introduction
The Identity Politics Trap

Welcome, reader, to the unapologetic exploration of one of the most polarizing figures in modern American politics – Kamala Harris. This book, "The BIGGEST Mistake America Will Make: Beyond Identity Politics: The Truth About Kamala Harris," is not just another political critique. It's a deep dive into the intricate web of identity politics that has ensnared our nation.

Identity politics, the practice of forming exclusive political alliances based on race, gender, and other aspects of identity, has become a double-edged sword in the American political landscape. It promises representation and empowerment, but it often delivers division and tokenism. This paradox is at the heart of our examination of Kamala Harris, a politician whose career has been both bolstered and besieged by the very identity markers she embodies.

Harris's rise to prominence is a classic American tale wrapped in the enigma of identity politics. Born to immigrant parents – an Indian mother and a Jamaican father – she stands as a testament to the

American dream. Yet, her political journey is fraught with the complexities and contradictions of identity politics. She has been celebrated as a trailblazer, the first woman, the first Black woman, and the first South Asian woman to serve as Vice President. But beneath these historic firsts lies a deeper, more troubling narrative.

Let's be clear − this book isn't about tearing down Kamala Harris. It's about unearthing the truths obscured by the glittering façade of identity politics. It's about asking the tough questions: Does Harris's identity truly represent progress for all, or is it a strategic guise employed by a political system eager to appear progressive while maintaining the status quo?

To understand the identity politics trap, we must first acknowledge its allure. In a nation riddled with historical and systemic injustices, the call for representation is not just valid – it's vital. Representation matters. Seeing oneself reflected in the halls of power can inspire hope and foster a sense of belonging. However, when representation becomes the sole criterion for leadership, we risk valuing appearance over substance, symbolism over real change.

Kamala Harris's career is a case study in this dynamic. Her ascent was not merely about her qualifications or her policies − it was about what she represented. For many, she symbolized a break from the old guard, a step towards a more inclusive America. But this symbolism often overshadowed a critical examination of her actual record and capabilities. This is the trap of identity politics − the focus shifts from the individual's actions and policies to their demographic characteristics.

Introduction

Harris's political journey has been marked by significant achievements and notable controversies. From her time as a prosecutor in San Francisco to her role as California's Attorney General, Harris has faced scrutiny for her tough-on-crime policies and handling of police misconduct cases. Her tenure as a U.S. Senator further showcased her ability to navigate the complexities of American politics, but it also highlighted inconsistencies in her policy positions and political strategy .

In this book, we will peel back the layers of Kamala Harris's political persona. We will scrutinize her record, question her leadership, and dissect the strategies that brought her to power. We will explore how identity politics has both aided and hindered her, and what this means for the future of American democracy.

Harris has leveraged her mixed-race identity to boost her political profile, challenging Democratic Party leaders on their relationship with minorities and advocating for greater representation of women of color in leadership roles. However, this has also led to accusations of tokenism and strategic manipulation of her identity for political gain .

As we embark on this journey, let's remember: the goal is not to vilify but to understand. To move beyond identity politics, we must engage with it critically and honestly. We must demand more than just representation; we must demand representation that leads to meaningful, equitable change. Kamala Harris's story is more than just a political biography; it's a mirror reflecting the strengths and weaknesses of identity politics in America.

Buckle up, reader. This is going to be an unfiltered, no-holds-barred exploration. We will leave no stone unturned and no question unasked. Welcome to the truth beyond identity politics. Welcome to "The BIGGEST Mistake America Will Make."

Chapter 1
Political Chess
The Machinations Behind Harris's Rise

Welcome to the high-stakes game of political chess, where every move is calculated, every alliance is strategic, and nothing is as it seems. In this chapter, we pull back the curtain on the intricate maneuvers and power plays that have defined Kamala Harris's political ascent. This isn't just politics as usual; it's a masterclass in ambition, strategy, and the ruthless pursuit of power.

Kamala Harris's rise in the political arena didn't happen by accident. It was the result of careful planning, opportunistic alliances, and a keen understanding of the political landscape. From her early days as a prosecutor in San Francisco to her current role as Vice President, Harris has navigated the murky waters of American politics with precision and intent.

. . .

Let's start at the beginning. Harris's career began in the San Francisco District Attorney's office, where she quickly made a name for herself. But it wasn't just her legal acumen that propelled her forward; it was her ability to leverage connections and forge alliances. Her relationship with influential figures like former San Francisco Mayor Willie Brown played a significant role in her early career. Brown, a powerful political figure, was instrumental in Harris's appointment to key state boards, which provided her with a platform to build her political brand .

Harris's tenure as District Attorney was marked by a mix of tough-on-crime policies and controversial decisions. She positioned herself as a progressive prosecutor, but her record tells a more complex story. While she implemented innovative programs aimed at reducing recidivism, she also faced criticism for her handling of cases involving police misconduct and her stance on the death penalty. These contradictions would later become focal points in her political narrative .

The next major leap in Harris's career came when she ran for California Attorney General in 2010. This race was a turning point, showcasing her strategic prowess. Despite being outspent and facing stiff competition, Harris won by a razor-thin margin. Her victory was a testament to her ability to mobilize support, particularly among minority communities and progressive voters. But behind the scenes, it was her network of political allies and her campaign's strategic targeting that made the difference .

·   ·   ·

As Attorney General, Harris continued to build her political capital. She tackled big banks in the wake of the foreclosure crisis, securing a $25 billion settlement for California homeowners. This move bolstered her image as a consumer advocate and a tough, no-nonsense prosecutor. However, her tenure was also marked by controversies, including her office's handling of wrongful conviction cases and her initial opposition to statewide police body camera mandates. These issues raised questions about her progressive credentials and fore-shadowed future critiques .

The leap to the national stage came in 2016, when Harris ran for the U.S. Senate. This campaign was a showcase of her political savvy. She secured endorsements from key figures like President Barack Obama and Vice President Joe Biden, leveraging their support to outmaneuver her opponents. Her victory in the Senate race cemented her status as a rising star in the Democratic Party .

In the Senate, Harris quickly made her mark. Her sharp questioning during Senate hearings, particularly her grilling of then-Attorney General Jeff Sessions and Supreme Court nominee Brett Kavanaugh, earned her national recognition. She positioned herself as a formidable opponent to the Trump administration, aligning with the progressive wing of the Democratic Party on issues like immigration, healthcare, and criminal justice reform .

But the true test of her political acumen came during the 2020 presidential primary. Harris's campaign started with great promise. Her launch event in

Oakland drew a massive crowd, and she was initially seen as a top-tier candidate. However, her campaign struggled with messaging and internal conflicts. The pivotal moment came during a primary debate when Harris attacked Joe Biden over his past opposition to federally mandated busing. This move was seen as a gamble – one that ultimately backfired as it alienated some voters and donors. Harris's campaign faltered, and she eventually withdrew from the race before the first primary votes were cast.

Yet, this setback was only temporary. Harris's endorsement of Biden and her subsequent selection as his running mate demonstrated her resilience and strategic foresight. Her vice-presidential nomination was the culmination of years of political maneuvering. It was a testament to her ability to navigate the complex dynamics of the Democratic Party and position herself as the ideal running mate for Biden, bridging the gap between the party's moderate and progressive factions.

Kamala Harris's rise is a story of calculated moves and strategic alliances. It's about understanding when to strike and when to step back. It's about leveraging relationships and positioning oneself at the right place at the right time. But it's also a story of contradictions and compromises, of progressive ideals clashing with pragmatic decisions.

In the game of political chess, Kamala Harris has proven herself to be a formidable player. Her ascent is a masterclass in ambition and strategy, offering a glimpse into the inner workings of American politics. As we continue to unravel her story, we'll see how these early maneuvers have shaped her path and what they mean for her future and the future of American politics.

Chapter 2
A Record Under Fire
Scrutinizing Harris's Legacy

Now that we've dissected the strategic moves that propelled Kamala Harris to power, it's time to turn our gaze to the heart of the matter – her record. The glowing endorsements, the high-profile positions, the historic firsts – they all sound impressive. But what happens when we peel back the layers and scrutinize the legacy she's built? Buckle up, because this chapter pulls no punches.

Kamala Harris's political career spans several key roles – San Francisco District Attorney, California Attorney General, U.S. Senator, and now Vice President. Each position comes with its own set of achievements and controversies, and together they paint a complex picture of her legacy.

Let's start with her tenure as San Francisco District Attorney. Harris took office in 2004, positioning herself

as a tough-on-crime prosecutor with a progressive twist. One of her notable initiatives was the "Back on Track" program, which offered first-time drug offenders a chance to avoid prison by completing a rigorous program that included job training and community service. This program was hailed as innovative and forward-thinking, aiming to reduce recidivism and give offenders a second chance.

However, her time as District Attorney wasn't without its controversies. Harris faced criticism for her office's handling of police misconduct cases. In 2010, a scandal erupted when it was revealed that a crime lab technician had been skimming cocaine from evidence samples, leading to the dismissal of hundreds of cases. Critics argued that Harris's office should have disclosed the technician's issues earlier, a failure that called into question her commitment to transparency and justice .

Harris's strategic manipulation of her conviction rates also came under fire. By prosecuting fewer cases and offering generous plea deals, Harris boosted her office's conviction rate on paper, but police officers felt betrayed as serious offenders were given lenient sentences . Her refusal to seek the death penalty for a cop killer further strained her relationship with law enforcement and sparked public outrage .

Moving on to her role as California Attorney General from 2011 to 2017, Harris continued to build her reputation as a tough, effective leader. She took on the big banks in the aftermath of the foreclosure crisis, securing a $25 billion settlement for California homeowners – a major win that showcased her ability to

stand up to powerful interests. She also implemented the Open Justice initiative, an online platform aimed at increasing transparency in the criminal justice system by making data on arrests, deaths in custody, and law enforcement practices publicly accessible.

But again, Harris's record was a mixed bag. Her office was criticized for defending convictions obtained through prosecutorial misconduct. One particularly damning case involved the failure to disclose a crime lab technician's history of false testimony, which led to the wrongful conviction of a man who spent years on death row . Additionally, her stance on the death penalty drew fire from both sides of the aisle – she personally opposed it but defended it in court, a position that seemed to straddle both sides without fully committing to either .

Harris's prosecution of parents for their children's truancy also garnered significant backlash. Her policy of threatening jail time and hefty fines for parents of truant children was criticized as overly punitive and indicative of her willingness to use the criminal justice system to enforce social policy .

Harris's time in the U.S. Senate further exemplified this pattern of progressive ideals clashing with pragmatic politics. She emerged as a vocal critic of the Trump administration, using her position on the Senate Judiciary Committee to challenge key figures like Jeff Sessions and Brett Kavanaugh. Her sharp, incisive questioning during these hearings earned her national acclaim and solidified her image as a fierce advocate for justice.

. . .

However, her legislative record was less impactful than her public persona might suggest. Harris introduced or co-sponsored several progressive bills, including the Marijuana Justice Act and the Maternal CARE Act, but many of these initiatives stalled in the Senate. Critics argue that while she talked the talk, she struggled to walk the walk, failing to push through substantial legislation that could translate her rhetoric into real change .

As Vice President, Harris has continued to face intense scrutiny. Her portfolio includes significant challenges such as immigration, voting rights, and managing the COVID-19 response. Her handling of the border crisis has been particularly controversial. Critics on the right accuse her of being too lenient, while those on the left argue that she hasn't done enough to address the humanitarian issues at the border. This balancing act reflects the broader tension in her political career – trying to satisfy both progressive and moderate wings of the Democratic Party without fully committing to either.

Her leadership on voting rights has also been a contentious issue. While she has been vocal about the importance of protecting and expanding voting rights, actual legislative victories have been hard to come by. The For the People Act and the John Lewis Voting Rights Advancement Act, both crucial pieces of legislation for the Democratic agenda, have faced significant hurdles in Congress. Harris's ability to navigate these challenges will be a critical test of her political acumen and leadership .

. . .

In summation, Kamala Harris's legacy is a study in contrasts. Her career is marked by groundbreaking achievements and significant controversies. She has championed progressive causes but often found herself mired in the complexities and compromises of realpolitik. Harris's record reflects the broader challenges of pursuing a progressive agenda within the constraints of American political institutions.

As we continue to examine her journey, keep in mind that every accolade and every critique serves to highlight the multifaceted nature of her career. Harris's story is not just about her; it's a mirror reflecting the larger issues within American politics – the struggle between ideals and practicality, the demands of representation versus the need for effective governance.

Stay with us as we delve deeper into the enigma that is Kamala Harris. Next up, we tackle her leadership qualities in Chapter 4: Leadership Under Siege: Can Harris Deliver?

Chapter 3
Leadership Under Siege
Can Harris Deliver?

Welcome to the crucible of American politics, where leaders are forged or broken. Kamala Harris has navigated the political labyrinth with skill and determination, but can she truly lead? This chapter dives into Harris's leadership style, challenges, and the relentless scrutiny she faces as Vice President. We will uncover whether she has what it takes to deliver on her promises and lead a divided nation.

Kamala Harris's ascent to the vice presidency is historic. As the first woman, first Black woman, and first South Asian woman to hold the office, her leadership is under intense scrutiny. But historic firsts come with heightened expectations and challenges. Harris's ability to lead is continuously tested by the political, social, and economic turbulence facing the nation.

. . .

Leadership isn't just about holding a title; it's about demonstrating capability, resilience, and vision. Harris's leadership style can be best described as pragmatic and adaptive. She combines a prosecutorial sharpness with a politician's instinct for survival. But this blend of qualities has been both a strength and a weakness, often leading to perceptions of inconsistency or opportunism.

During her time as California Attorney General, Harris exhibited a hands-on leadership approach. She implemented several forward-thinking initiatives, such as the creation of OpenJustice, a data-driven effort to improve transparency in the criminal justice system. Her decision to confront big banks and secure a $25 billion settlement for California homeowners showcased her willingness to take on powerful interests. These moves highlighted her ability to lead from the front, setting ambitious goals and driving them to fruition.

However, Harris's leadership has also faced significant challenges and criticisms. Her handling of contentious issues like the death penalty and police misconduct raised questions about her ability to take definitive stances. As Attorney General, she faced backlash for not taking a stronger position against the death penalty, despite her personal opposition to it. This hesitation was perceived as a political calculation, aimed at avoiding alienation of certain voter blocs .

As Vice President, Harris's leadership is under even more intense scrutiny. One of her primary responsibilities has been addressing the immigration crisis at the southern border. This role has proven to be a baptism by fire, with Harris caught between the demands for

humane immigration policies and the pressures to enforce border security. Critics argue that her response has been tepid and reactive, rather than bold and proactive.

Harris's approach to immigration reflects a broader challenge in her leadership style – the struggle to balance progressive ideals with political pragmatism. Her reluctance to fully embrace one side over the other has sometimes resulted in criticism from both ends of the political spectrum. Progressives demand more decisive action on issues like immigration and criminal justice reform, while moderates and conservatives seek stronger enforcement measures and clarity in policy .

Her handling of the COVID-19 pandemic response is another critical area of her vice presidency. As part of the Biden administration, Harris has been involved in the rollout of vaccination programs and public health initiatives. While the administration has made significant strides in increasing vaccination rates and managing the pandemic, the effort has not been without its pitfalls. Mixed messaging and logistical challenges have sometimes overshadowed the progress made, and Harris's role in these efforts is frequently scrutinized.

One of the defining moments of Harris's vice presidency came when she took the lead on voting rights. Tasked with protecting and expanding access to the ballot, Harris has been vocal about the threats to democracy posed by restrictive voting laws. Her speeches have been impassioned, calling for federal legislation to counteract state-level efforts to limit voting access. However, the legislative victories in this area have been elusive, raising questions about her effectiveness in marshaling support and overcoming political obstacles .

In the Senate, Harris was known for her incisive questioning and sharp rhetoric during high-profile hearings. This prosecutorial approach earned her praise and spotlight, but it also drew criticism for being too confrontational. As Vice President, Harris has had to adapt her style, working more behind the scenes and building coalitions. This shift from a front-line interrogator to a consensus-building leader has been challenging, highlighting the difficulties of transitioning between different roles in government.

Leadership under siege isn't just about external pressures; it's also about internal dynamics. Harris has faced reports of discord within her team, with staff turnover and allegations of a toxic work environment. These internal challenges reflect the broader difficulties of managing a high-pressure political office, where the stakes are incredibly high and the scrutiny unrelenting .

Harris's leadership journey is a testament to the complexities of modern politics. She has shown moments of brilliance and resilience, but she has also faced significant hurdles that test her capabilities. Her ability to navigate these challenges will be crucial in determining whether she can deliver on her promises and lead effectively.

· · ·

In conclusion, Kamala Harris's leadership is a work in progress, characterized by a blend of pragmatism, ambition, and the ever-present tension between idealism and reality. She stands at a critical juncture, with the potential to shape the future of American politics. The question remains – can she rise to the occasion and lead a nation through its most trying times? Only time will tell, but one thing is certain: the scrutiny and expectations will not wane.

Stay with us as we continue to peel back the layers of Kamala Harris's career. Next, we delve into a sensitive and crucial topic in Chapter 5: Exploiting Black Voters: The Ultimate Betrayal.

Chapter 4
Exploiting Black Voters
The Ultimate Betrayal

Buckle up, folks. We're diving into one of the most controversial and contentious topics in American politics – the exploitation of Black voters. Kamala Harris, with her historic rise, has often been portrayed as a champion of the Black community. But has this narrative been used to manipulate and exploit the very people she claims to represent? This chapter exposes the hard truths and uncomfortable realities behind the politics of representation.

Kamala Harris's identity as a Black woman has been central to her political brand. Her Jamaican heritage, coupled with her career as a prosecutor and politician, positioned her as a symbol of progress and representation for Black Americans. But this symbolism, while powerful, has often masked a more complex and troubling reality.

· · ·

Let's start with the basics. Representation matters. It's vital for young Black Americans to see themselves reflected in positions of power. It inspires hope and a sense of possibility. But when representation is reduced to mere optics, it becomes a tool for political manipulation. Harris's political journey is rife with instances where her identity has been leveraged to secure votes without necessarily delivering on the substantive issues that affect the Black community.

During her campaign for the Democratic nomination, Harris often invoked her background to connect with Black voters. Her personal story of growing up as a Black woman in America was a central theme in her speeches. She frequently spoke about her experiences with racism and the lessons she learned from her parents about justice and activism. These narratives resonated with many voters, creating a sense of shared identity and common struggle.

However, Harris's record as a prosecutor and Attorney General paints a different picture. While she has implemented some progressive reforms, her tenure was also marked by policies that disproportionately impacted Black communities. Her office's aggressive stance on truancy, for example, led to the prosecution of parents whose children missed school – a policy that critics argue criminalized poverty and disproportionately affected Black families.

In her role as California Attorney General, Harris's handling of police misconduct cases drew significant criticism. Despite high-profile incidents of police violence against Black individuals, her office was often slow to act. For instance, her reluctance to support

statewide mandates for body cameras on police officers and her defense of controversial police practices raised questions about her commitment to justice for Black communities. These actions created a stark contrast to her campaign rhetoric about reforming the criminal justice system.

Harris's vice-presidential nomination was seen as a historic win for representation. Yet, the Biden-Harris campaign's approach to Black voters often felt transactional. The campaign heavily courted Black voters, especially in key swing states, emphasizing Harris's identity and her potential to break barriers. This strategy worked to an extent – the high turnout among Black voters in places like Georgia and Pennsylvania was crucial to Biden's victory.

But once the election was won, many Black voters felt their concerns were sidelined. The promise of police reform, voting rights protections, and economic justice – issues central to the Black community – faced significant delays and political hurdles. The administration's struggles to pass substantial legislation in these areas led to feelings of betrayal and frustration among the very voters who had been instrumental in their electoral success.

The exploitation of Black voters isn't just about broken promises; it's also about the deeper issue of using identity politics as a shield against legitimate criticism. Harris's defenders often invoke her identity to deflect critiques of her policies, labeling dissent as racially motivated or sexist. This tactic not only stifles meaningful debate but also undermines the very principles of accountability and transparency that are essential for effective governance.

Moreover, the Biden-Harris administration's handling of key issues impacting Black communities has been inconsistent at best. The response to the Black Lives Matter movement, for instance, has been tepid. While Harris participated in marches and made statements supporting the movement, the administration's legislative follow-through has been lacking. The George Floyd Justice in Policing Act, a critical piece of police reform legislation, has stalled in Congress, highlighting the gap between rhetoric and action.

The use of Kamala Harris's identity in political marketing also raises ethical questions. Is it fair to present her as the embodiment of progress for Black Americans when her record and policies tell a more complicated story? The answer isn't straightforward, but it's a question that deserves honest exploration.

In conclusion, the exploitation of Black voters through the politics of representation is a significant issue in Kamala Harris's political career. While her rise is undoubtedly historic and inspirational, it's essential to look beyond the surface and critically examine whether her actions have matched her promises. Representation is crucial, but it must be coupled with substantive policies and genuine accountability. Otherwise, it risks becoming a tool for manipulation rather than a catalyst for real change.

. . .

Stay tuned as we continue this deep dive into the truth behind Kamala Harris's political journey. Next, we'll explore the Democratic primary that never really happened in Chapter 6: "The Sham Primary: Where Was the Debate?"

Chapter 5
The Sham Primary
Where Was the Debate?

Welcome to the backstage of the 2024 Democratic primary – a political spectacle that promised rigorous debate and diverse voices but delivered a tightly controlled narrative. In this chapter, we uncover how the primary process was manipulated, stifling genuine discourse and debate. Buckle up, because this is where we pull back the curtain on the orchestrated theater of modern American politics.

The 2024 Democratic primary has turned out to be more of a coronation than a competition. With President Joe Biden stepping out of the race just four months before Election Day, his endorsement of Kamala Harris as the Democratic nominee has all but sealed the deal. This maneuver has effectively shut down any chance for a genuine primary contest, leaving many Democrats frustrated and disenfranchised .

. . .

When Biden announced his decision to step aside, the expectation was that the Democratic Party would open the floor for a robust debate, giving other potential candidates a chance to present their visions for the future. Instead, the endorsement of Harris felt like a predetermined outcome, orchestrated to maintain the status quo rather than embracing the democratic process .

From the outset, it was clear that the Democratic establishment had its favorites. Harris, with her extensive political resume and ties to the Biden administration, was the presumed front-runner. The media coverage and party support she received reinforced her status as the candidate to beat. This was reminiscent of the 2020 primary, where Joe Biden was similarly positioned as the inevitable nominee.

Harris's campaign launch in Oakland was a spectacle of its own. With thousands of supporters in attendance and a powerful speech that highlighted her vision for America, Harris positioned herself as a top-tier candidate. Her early polling numbers were strong, and she seemed poised to be a serious contender. But as the primary progressed, the dynamics shifted, revealing the underbelly of the political process .

The infamous debate where Harris confronted Biden on his past opposition to federally mandated busing is still fresh in the minds of many. The exchange was intense and made headlines, but it also marked a turning point for Harris's campaign. While the confrontation was meant to highlight Biden's problematic history on civil rights, it backfired, alienating some voters and donors who viewed it as an unfair attack on a beloved party figure.

The fallout from this debate underscored a critical issue in the primary – the lack of genuine, substantive debate on the issues. Instead of fostering a platform for diverse voices and perspectives, the primary became a battleground for personal attacks and superficial soundbites. The media's focus on these sensational moments detracted from meaningful discussions about policy and vision for the country .

Harris's campaign struggled to maintain momentum in this environment. Despite her strong debate performances and compelling personal story, her campaign faced internal strife and messaging inconsistencies. Reports of infighting and strategic missteps plagued her efforts, ultimately leading to her withdrawal from the race before the first primary votes were even cast .

But Harris wasn't the only casualty of this orchestrated primary. Progressive candidates like Bernie Sanders and Elizabeth Warren, who brought bold ideas and substantial policy proposals to the table, found themselves marginalized by the party establishment. The primary process seemed designed to consolidate support around a centrist candidate, stifling the progressive movement that had gained significant traction among the Democratic base .

The role of the Democratic National Committee (DNC) in shaping the primary outcome cannot be overlooked. The DNC's debate rules, fundraising thresholds, and delegate allocation processes played a significant role in narrowing the field and influencing voter perception. Candidates who struggled to meet these thresholds, regardless of their policy ideas or grassroots support, were effectively silenced.

The media's complicity in this process was equally damaging. Instead of providing a platform for a diverse range of ideas, major media outlets often focused on sensationalism and horse-race coverage. This approach not only skewed public perception but also reinforced the establishment's narrative, leaving little room for genuine debate and critical discussion .

Harris's eventual endorsement of Biden and her selection as his running mate highlighted the strategic alliances and political maneuvering that defined the primary. Her decision to support Biden, despite their earlier clash, was a calculated move that aligned her with the party's establishment. It also underscored the transactional nature of modern politics, where alliances are often based on expediency rather than shared ideals.

The 2024 Democratic primary has turned out to be a missed opportunity for the party to engage in a meaningful dialogue about its future. Instead of embracing the diversity of thought and experience within its ranks, the primary process was manipulated to produce a predetermined outcome. This approach not only disenfranchised many voters but also undermined the very principles of democracy and fair competition .

. . .

In conclusion, the 2024 Democratic primary was a sham – a carefully orchestrated spectacle that stifled genuine debate and manipulated voter choice. Kamala Harris's journey through this process is emblematic of the broader issues within American politics. Her rise and fall in the primary highlight the challenges faced by candidates who dare to challenge the establishment narrative.

As we move forward, it's essential to recognize these manipulations and demand a more transparent and democratic primary process. Only then can we ensure that the voices of all voters and candidates are heard and respected.

Stay with us as we continue to explore the complexities of Kamala Harris's political career. Next, we delve into the broader implications of identity politics in Chapter 7: **Identity Politics: Unity or Division?**

Chapter 6
Exploiting Black Voters
The Ultimate Betrayal

Buckle up, folks. We're diving into one of the most controversial and contentious topics in American politics – the exploitation of Black voters. Kamala Harris, with her historic rise, has often been portrayed as a champion of the Black community. But has this narrative been used to manipulate and exploit the very people she claims to represent? This chapter exposes the hard truths and uncomfortable realities behind the politics of representation.

Kamala Harris's identity as a Black woman has been central to her political brand. Her Jamaican heritage, coupled with her career as a prosecutor and politician, positioned her as a symbol of progress and representation for Black Americans. But this symbolism, while powerful, has often masked a more complex and troubling reality.

Let's start with the basics. Representation matters. It's vital for young Black Americans to see themselves reflected in positions of power. It inspires hope and a sense of possibility. But when representation is reduced to mere optics, it becomes a tool for political manipulation. Harris's political journey is rife with instances where her identity has been leveraged to secure votes without necessarily delivering on the substantive issues that affect the Black community.

During her campaign for the Democratic nomination, Harris often invoked her background to connect with Black voters. Her personal story of growing up as a Black woman in America was a central theme in her speeches. She frequently spoke about her experiences with racism and the lessons she learned from her parents about justice and activism. These narratives resonated with many voters, creating a sense of shared identity and common struggle.

However, Harris's record as a prosecutor and Attorney General paints a different picture. While she has implemented some progressive reforms, her tenure was also marked by policies that disproportionately impacted Black communities. Her office's aggressive stance on truancy, for example, led to the prosecution of parents whose children missed school – a policy that critics argue criminalized poverty and disproportionately affected Black families .

In her role as California Attorney General, Harris's handling of police misconduct cases drew significant criticism. Despite high-profile incidents of police violence against Black individuals, her office was often slow to act. For instance, her reluctance to support statewide mandates for body cameras on police officers and her defense of controversial police practices raised questions about her commitment to justice for Black communities. These actions created a stark contrast to her campaign rhetoric about reforming the criminal justice system .

. . .

Harris's vice-presidential nomination was seen as a historic win for representation. Yet, the Biden-Harris campaign's approach to Black voters often felt transactional. The campaign heavily courted Black voters, especially in key swing states, emphasizing Harris's identity and her potential to break barriers. This strategy worked to an extent – the high turnout among Black voters in places like Georgia and Pennsylvania was crucial to Biden's victory .

But once the election was won, many Black voters felt their concerns were sidelined. The promise of police reform, voting rights protections, and economic justice – issues central to the Black community – faced significant delays and political hurdles. The administration's struggles to pass substantial legislation in these areas led to feelings of betrayal and frustration among the very voters who had been instrumental in their electoral success .

The exploitation of Black voters isn't just about broken promises; it's also about the deeper issue of using identity politics as a shield against legitimate criticism. Harris's defenders often invoke her identity to deflect critiques of her policies, labeling dissent as racially motivated or sexist. This tactic not only stifles meaningful debate but also undermines the very principles of accountability and transparency that are essential for effective governance .

Moreover, the Biden-Harris administration's handling of key issues impacting Black communities has been inconsistent at best. The response to the Black Lives Matter movement, for instance, has been tepid. While Harris participated in marches and made statements supporting the movement, the administration's legislative follow-through has been lacking. The George Floyd Justice in Policing Act, a critical piece of police reform legislation, has stalled in Congress, highlighting the gap between rhetoric and action .

The use of Kamala Harris's identity in political marketing also raises ethical questions. Is it fair to present her as the embodiment of progress for Black Americans when her record and policies tell a more complicated story? The answer isn't straightforward, but it's a question that deserves honest exploration.

In conclusion, the exploitation of Black voters through the politics of representation is a significant issue in Kamala Harris's political career. While her rise is undoubtedly historic and inspirational, it's essential to look beyond the surface and critically examine whether her actions have matched her promises. Representation is crucial, but it must be coupled with substantive policies and genuine accountability. Otherwise, it risks becoming a tool for manipulation rather than a catalyst for real change.

Stay tuned as we continue this deep dive into the truth behind Kamala Harris's political journey. Next, we'll explore the Democratic primary that never really happened in Chapter 6: "The Sham Primary: Where Was the Debate?"

Chapter 7
The Gender and Race Card
Political Ploys Unveiled

Politics is a game of strategy, and few strategies are as powerful—or as controversial—as the use of gender and race. In this chapter, we rip the veil off the calculated deployment of these identity markers in Kamala Harris's career. We'll dissect how these elements have been used as both a shield and a sword in her political journey. Prepare yourself for an unflinching look at the political machinations behind the façade of identity.

Kamala Harris's rise to power is undeniably historic. Her identity as a Black and South Asian woman has been a cornerstone of her political narrative. From her early days in California politics to her current role as Vice President, Harris has consistently leveraged her identity to build a broad coalition of supporters. But this strategy, while effective in many ways, has also invited criticism and scrutiny.

First, let's acknowledge the power of representation. Seeing a woman of color in one of the highest offices in the land is profoundly significant for many Americans. It symbolizes progress and the breaking of barriers that have long excluded marginalized groups from positions of power. Harris's story resonates with countless individuals who see their own struggles and aspirations reflected in her journey.

However, the use of gender and race in political campaigns is a double-edged sword. While it can inspire and mobilize, it can also be perceived as a cynical ploy to garner votes without addressing the substantive issues that affect those very communities. Harris's career provides a clear example of this dynamic at play.

During her run for California Attorney General, Harris's campaign emphasized her identity as a progressive Black woman committed to justice. This narrative helped her connect with minority voters who were eager for representation. Yet, her record as Attorney General reveals a more complex story. Harris's office defended controversial policies that disproportionately affected Black and brown communities, such as the prosecution of parents for their children's truancy. These actions raised questions about whether her policies truly aligned with the progressive values she espoused.

The 2020 Democratic primary brought these issues into sharper focus. Harris's campaign launch was a masterclass in the strategic use of identity. Her announcement in Oakland, a city with deep historical ties to the civil rights movement, was a powerful statement. She framed her candidacy as a continuation of the fight for justice and equality, invoking the legacy of leaders like Martin Luther King Jr. and Shirley Chisholm. However, her attempt to challenge Joe Biden on his past opposition to federally mandated busing was a bold move meant to highlight her commitment to civil rights. Instead, it backfired, appearing opportunistic and divisive, ultimately contributing to her campaign's decline.

As Vice President, Harris's identity continues to be a focal point. The Biden-Harris administration has frequently highlighted the historic nature of her role, using it to signal a commitment to diversity and inclusion. However, the administration's handling of key issues like immigration and police reform has drawn criticism from activists and community leaders who feel that symbolic representation has not translated into meaningful action.

One of the most contentious aspects of Harris's identity politics is the perception that it is used to deflect criticism. When faced with scrutiny over her record or decisions, her defenders often frame the critiques as racially or gender-motivated attacks. While it is undeniable that racism and sexism play a role in the treatment of women of color in politics, this tactic can also stifle legitimate debate and accountability.

The strategic use of gender and race extends beyond Harris's personal narrative to the broader Democratic Party's electoral strategy. The 2020 election saw a concerted effort to appeal to women and minority voters, with Harris as a key figure in this approach. The campaign's messaging frequently highlighted her identity, aiming to mobilize these demographics. This strategy was effective in many respects, contributing to high voter turnout among Black and minority communities.

However, the reliance on identity markers also risks alienating other voters who feel that their concerns are overlooked. The focus on representation must be balanced with substantive policy discussions that address the needs of all Americans. Failure to do so can create a perception of tokenism, where candidates are seen as symbols rather than effective leaders.

In conclusion, the deployment of gender and race in Kamala Harris's political career is a nuanced and multifaceted strategy. It has been instrumental in her rise to power, providing a source of inspiration and connection for many voters. Yet, it also raises critical questions about the nature of representation and the balance between symbolic and substantive politics.

As we continue our exploration of Kamala Harris's career, it's essential to remain vigilant about the promises and pitfalls of identity politics. Representation is vital, but it must be coupled with genuine accountability and policy action.

Join us next as we delve deeper into Kamala Harris's political agenda and the reality behind her public persona in Chapter 9: Behind the Mask: Harris's Real Agenda.

Chapter 8
Behind the Mask
Harris's Real Agenda

Get ready to pull back the curtain and uncover the true political agenda of Kamala Harris. Behind the polished speeches and carefully crafted image lies a complex set of beliefs, strategies, and policy goals that define her approach to governance. This chapter dives deep into Harris's real agenda, exploring her priorities, her ideological leanings, and the often-contradictory nature of her political philosophy.

Kamala Harris is a politician who defies easy categorization. Her career has been marked by a blend of progressive rhetoric and pragmatic decision-making, creating a sometimes confusing picture of where she truly stands on key issues. To understand Harris's real agenda, we must dissect her actions, policies, and public statements across her various roles.

As San Francisco District Attorney, Harris's agenda was shaped by a mix of tough-on-crime policies and progressive reforms. One of her notable initiatives was the "Back on Track" program, designed to reduce recidivism by providing first-time drug offenders with job training and education instead of prison time. This program reflected her belief in rehabilitation and second chances. However, her office also pursued aggressive prosecutions and upheld controversial policies that disproportionately impacted minority communities. This duality highlighted a tension between her progressive aspirations and the realities of the criminal justice system.

Harris's tenure as California Attorney General further illustrated her complex political philosophy. She positioned herself as a consumer advocate, taking on big banks in the aftermath of the foreclosure crisis and securing a significant settlement for homeowners. Her commitment to transparency was evident in the creation of the OpenJustice initiative, which aimed to increase accountability in law enforcement. Yet, her office also defended convictions obtained through prosecutorial misconduct and resisted calls for greater oversight of police practices. These actions revealed a pragmatic approach to governance, balancing progressive ideals with institutional constraints .

In the U.S. Senate, Harris continued to navigate this delicate balance. She emerged as a vocal critic of the Trump administration, using her platform on the Senate Judiciary Committee to challenge nominees and administration officials. Her sharp questioning of figures like Jeff Sessions and Brett Kavanaugh earned her national recognition and solidified her reputation as a fierce advocate for justice. But beyond these high-profile moments, her legislative record was more nuanced. Harris introduced and co-sponsored progressive bills on issues like criminal justice reform, healthcare, and economic equality, yet many of these initiatives faced significant hurdles in a divided Congress .

. . .

The 2020 presidential primary provided a closer look at Harris's political priorities and her ability to communicate a cohesive agenda. Her campaign platform included ambitious proposals on healthcare, climate change, and economic reform. She advocated for "Medicare for All," the Green New Deal, and significant investments in education and infrastructure. However, her campaign struggled with consistency, and her shifting positions on key issues led to accusations of political opportunism. For example, her stance on healthcare evolved from full support for "Medicare for All" to a more moderate approach, reflecting a pragmatic adjustment to political realities .

As Vice President, Harris's agenda has been shaped by the broader goals of the Biden administration. She has been tasked with addressing some of the most challenging issues facing the country, including immigration, voting rights, and the COVID-19 response. Her approach to these issues has been measured, often reflecting the administration's cautious strategy. On immigration, Harris has faced criticism from both the left and the right, with some accusing her of not doing enough to address the humanitarian crisis at the border, while others argue that her policies are too lenient .

Her leadership on voting rights has been a focal point of her vice presidency. Harris has passionately advocated for federal legislation to protect and expand access to the ballot, highlighting the ongoing threats to democracy posed by restrictive voting laws. Despite her efforts, significant legislative victories have been elusive, underscoring the challenges of navigating a polarized political landscape .

. . .

One of the defining aspects of Harris's political philosophy is her focus on equity and inclusion. Throughout her career, she has emphasized the importance of addressing systemic inequalities and promoting social justice. This commitment is evident in her advocacy for criminal justice reform, her support for policies aimed at reducing economic disparity, and her vocal defense of civil rights. However, translating these ideals into concrete policies has often been complicated by political opposition and institutional inertia.

Harris's real agenda is also shaped by her background and personal experiences. As the daughter of immigrants and a woman of color, her perspectives on issues like immigration, education, and healthcare are informed by her own journey. She frequently speaks about the influence of her mother, an activist and researcher, and her upbringing in a diverse community. These personal narratives are woven into her political rhetoric, reinforcing her commitment to representing marginalized voices .

In conclusion, Kamala Harris's real agenda is a blend of progressive aspirations and pragmatic governance. Her career is marked by a commitment to equity and justice, tempered by the realities of political compromise. She strives to balance bold policy proposals with the need to navigate complex political landscapes, making her a figure of both inspiration and contention.

As we continue to explore the intricacies of her political journey, we'll examine her policy successes and failures in greater detail. Join us next in Chapter 10: Progressive or Pretender? Harris's Policy Pitfalls, where we scrutinize the effectiveness of her policy initiatives and their alignment with her stated ideals.

Chapter 9
Progressive or Pretender?
Harris's Policy Pitfalls

The label of "progressive" carries with it a heavy burden of expectations – expectations of bold reforms, unwavering advocacy for marginalized communities, and a relentless pursuit of justice and equality. Kamala Harris has often been cast in this role, but does she truly live up to it? Or is she merely a pretender, using progressive rhetoric to mask more centrist policies? In this chapter, we dive deep into Harris's policy initiatives, successes, and shortcomings to uncover the truth.

Kamala Harris has made numerous claims to progressive ideals throughout her career. From her time as San Francisco District Attorney to her role as Vice President, she has championed causes that resonate with progressive voters. But examining her record reveals a more complex reality, filled with significant accomplishments as well as notable pitfalls.

· · ·

As San Francisco District Attorney, Harris implemented several programs that aligned with progressive values. The "Back on Track" initiative, which aimed to reduce recidivism by providing first-time drug offenders with education and job training, was a forward-thinking approach that sought to address the root causes of crime rather than merely punishing offenders. This program was a success in many respects, helping numerous individuals avoid the revolving door of the criminal justice system .

However, Harris's overall record as District Attorney was not without controversy. Her office's handling of police misconduct cases often fell short of progressive expectations. For instance, her decision not to support independent investigations into police shootings and her office's failure to disclose critical information about police officers with histories of misconduct drew significant criticism . These actions called into question her commitment to the accountability and transparency that are cornerstones of progressive justice reform.

Harris's tenure as California Attorney General provided further insight into her policy priorities and the challenges she faced in implementing them. One of her notable achievements was the creation of the OpenJustice initiative, an online platform designed to increase transparency in law enforcement by providing public access to data on arrests, deaths in custody, and other critical metrics. This initiative was widely praised as a significant step towards greater accountability in the criminal justice system .

Yet, Harris's record as Attorney General also included policies that clashed with progressive values. Her defense of the death penalty, despite her personal opposition to it, and her office's resistance to calls for the adoption of body cameras for police officers were seen as significant setbacks . Additionally, her aggressive prosecution of parents for their children's truancy was criticized as a policy that disproportionately affected low-income and minority communities, raising questions about her approach to justice and equity .

As a U.S. Senator, Harris introduced and co-sponsored numerous bills aimed at addressing key progressive issues. She was a vocal advocate for criminal justice reform, co-sponsoring the Marijuana Justice Act, which sought to decriminalize marijuana at the federal level and expunge the records of those convicted of marijuana-related offenses. She also introduced the Maternal CARE Act, aimed at addressing racial disparities in maternal health outcomes. These initiatives demonstrated her commitment to addressing systemic inequalities and promoting social justice .

However, many of Harris's legislative efforts faced significant obstacles and did not become law. Her support for "Medicare for All" initially garnered attention, but she later shifted to a more moderate stance, proposing a plan that maintained a role for private insurance. This shift was seen by some as a pragmatic adjustment to political realities, but by others as a betrayal of progressive principles. The inconsistency in her policy positions has fueled criticism that she is more of a political opportunist than a steadfast progressive .

Harris's role as Vice President has continued to highlight the complexities of her policy agenda. Tasked with addressing immigration, voting rights, and the COVID-19 pandemic, her performance has been closely scrutinized. On immigration, her emphasis on addressing the root causes of migration through economic and security aid to Central American countries reflects a long-term, structural approach. However, her handling of the border crisis has been criticized as inadequate by both progressives and conservatives .

Her leadership on voting rights has faced similar challenges. Despite her passionate advocacy for federal legislation to protect voting rights, significant legislative victories have been elusive. The For the People Act and the John Lewis Voting Rights Advancement Act, both critical to the Democratic agenda, have faced substantial opposition in Congress, highlighting the difficulties of translating progressive ideals into concrete policy achievements .

One of the central critiques of Harris's policy approach is the gap between her rhetoric and her actions. While she often speaks eloquently about the need for justice, equity, and reform, her policy record is mixed. This gap has led to perceptions that she is willing to adopt progressive stances when convenient but lacks the consistency and follow-through needed to enact lasting change .

In conclusion, Kamala Harris's policy record reveals a complex interplay between progressive aspirations and political pragmatism. Her initiatives like the "Back on Track" program and the OpenJustice initiative reflect a genuine commitment to reform and social justice. However, her controversial stances on issues like police misconduct, the death penalty, and her shifting positions on healthcare highlight the difficulties of maintaining a consistent progressive agenda within the constraints of political reality.

Harris's tenure as Vice President further underscores these challenges. While she has passionately advocated for progressive causes, such as voting rights and immigration reform, the lack of significant legislative victories points to the broader systemic obstacles she faces. The Biden-Harris administration's cautious approach often contrasts sharply with the bold rhetoric of the campaign trail, leaving many progressives frustrated and disillusioned .

So, is Kamala Harris a true progressive or merely a pretender? The answer isn't black and white. Harris embodies the tensions and contradictions inherent in American politics today. She is a politician striving to balance her progressive ideals with the practicalities of governance in a deeply divided nation. Her journey reflects the broader struggle of the Democratic Party to reconcile its diverse base and deliver on its promises of change.

As we continue our exploration of Harris's political career, it's crucial to recognize these complexities and the broader context in which she operates. The next chapter will delve into her legislative record in more detail, offering a critical analysis of her successes and failures in enacting meaningful change.

Join us next in Chapter 11: Harris's Legislative Failures: A Deep Dive, where we examine her performance in the Senate and her ability to translate her progressive rhetoric into tangible policy outcomes.

Chapter 10
Harris's Legislative Failures
A Deep Dive

Strap in, folks, because it's time to dig deep into the nitty-gritty of Kamala Harris's legislative record. This chapter isn't about glossing over failures or highlighting successes—it's about getting real with the hard facts. We're going to scrutinize her time in the Senate, exposing the gaps between her progressive promises and the actual legislative outcomes. If you thought politics was all about grand speeches and lofty ideals, think again. This is where the rubber meets the road.

Kamala Harris entered the U.S. Senate in 2017 with significant fanfare and expectations. Her background as a prosecutor and her growing national profile positioned her as a rising star within the Democratic Party. As a Senator, she was vocal on numerous issues, positioning herself as a progressive champion. But how did this rhetoric translate into legislative action?

. . .

One of Harris's early legislative efforts was the **Marijuana Justice Act**, which she co-sponsored with Senator Cory Booker. This bill aimed to decriminalize marijuana at the federal level, expunge the records of those convicted of marijuana-related offenses, and reinvest in communities most affected by the war on drugs. The act was bold and ambitious, aligning perfectly with progressive goals of criminal justice reform and racial equity. However, despite its promise, the bill failed to gain the necessary traction in a Republican-controlled Senate.

Similarly, Harris introduced the **Maternal CARE Act**, targeting racial disparities in maternal health outcomes. The bill proposed grants to address implicit bias in healthcare, support for innovative maternal health programs, and enhanced data collection on maternal health. While it garnered attention and highlighted a critical issue, the bill did not advance beyond committee discussions, reflecting the broader challenge of pushing progressive legislation through a divided Congress.

Harris's support for "Medicare for All" was another significant aspect of her legislative agenda. Initially, she co-sponsored Bernie Sanders' "Medicare for All" bill, signaling strong support for comprehensive healthcare reform. However, as her presidential campaign progressed, Harris modified her stance, proposing a more moderate plan that maintained a role for private insurance. This shift was seen as a pragmatic move to appeal to a broader electorate, but by others as a betrayal of progressive principles. The lack of a unified healthcare reform agenda among Democrats further hampered legislative progress in this area.

· · ·

In the realm of criminal justice reform, Harris co-sponsored the **Justice in Policing Act**, introduced in response to the George Floyd protests. The bill sought to address police misconduct and racial bias, banning chokeholds, limiting qualified immunity for police officers, and creating a national database to track police misconduct. Despite widespread support among Democrats and significant public pressure, the bill stalled in the Senate, underscoring the deep partisan divides over policing and criminal justice issues.

Voting rights have been another critical area of Harris's legislative focus. As Vice President, she has been tasked with leading the administration's efforts to protect and expand voting access. This includes advocating for the **For the People Act** and the **John Lewis Voting Rights Advancement Act**. Both pieces of legislation aim to counteract state-level efforts to restrict voting access, enhance voter registration, and reduce the influence of money in politics. Despite her passionate advocacy, these bills have faced significant opposition from Republicans, making their passage uncertain.

Harris's legislative record also includes efforts to address climate change, gun control, and economic inequality. She co-sponsored the **Green New Deal** resolution, supporting a comprehensive approach to tackling climate change and transitioning to a green economy. Her advocacy for stricter gun control measures included co-sponsoring bills to expand background checks and close loopholes in gun sales. On economic issues, Harris introduced the **LIFT the Middle Class Act**, proposing tax credits to provide financial relief to low- and middle-income families.

Despite these efforts, Harris's legislative achievements have been limited. The challenges she faced highlight the broader difficulties of enacting progressive policies in a polarized political environment. The need for bipartisan support, the influence of special interest groups, and the complexities of the legislative process often stymie even the most well-intentioned efforts.

One of the recurring themes in Harris's legislative career is the tension between her progressive aspirations and the pragmatic realities of governance. While she has championed bold initiatives and articulated a vision for a more equitable and just society, the path to realizing these goals has been fraught with obstacles. This tension has led to perceptions that she is more adept at articulating progressive ideals than at enacting them.

In conclusion, Kamala Harris's legislative record is a testament to the complexities of American politics. Her efforts to push progressive legislation have often been thwarted by institutional barriers and partisan opposition. While she has introduced and supported numerous bills aimed at addressing systemic injustices and promoting social equity, the tangible outcomes have been limited. This gap between ambition and achievement raises critical questions about the effectiveness of her legislative strategy and the broader challenges facing progressive lawmakers.

As we continue to dissect Harris's political journey, it's crucial to understand these legislative failures in context. They reflect not just on Harris but on the systemic hurdles that impede meaningful reform in the U.S. political system. Join us next in Chapter 12: **Voter Deception: Substance or Symbolism?**, where we explore the critical issue of voter perception and the gap between political rhetoric and reality.

Chapter 11
Voter Deception
Substance or Symbolism?

Welcome to the heart of political theater – where perception often trumps reality and symbolism can overshadow substance. In this chapter, we dissect the delicate dance of voter perception, exploring how politicians like Kamala Harris navigate the tricky waters of public image versus actual policy impact. Are voters being deceived by the allure of representation, or is there genuine substance behind the symbols? Let's pull back the curtain and find out.

Kamala Harris's political career is a masterclass in the power of symbolism. Her rise to the vice presidency is historic, breaking multiple barriers and setting a new precedent for diversity in American politics. Her identity as a Black and South Asian woman has been central to her appeal, resonating deeply with voters who see her as a symbol of progress and inclusion. But beneath this powerful symbolism lies a critical question: how much of Harris's appeal is based on substance, and how much is rooted in the symbolism of her identity?

. . .

The power of representation cannot be overstated. For many voters, seeing someone who looks like them in a position of power is profoundly inspiring. Harris's identity and personal story – as the daughter of immigrants, a graduate of historically Black Howard University, and a former prosecutor – embody the American dream. This narrative has been skillfully woven into her political campaigns, creating a powerful connection with voters, particularly those from marginalized communities .

However, the focus on representation can sometimes obscure a deeper examination of a politician's record and policies. In Harris's case, her identity has often been at the forefront of her public image, sometimes at the expense of substantive policy discussions. This emphasis on symbolism raises important questions about voter perception and the potential for deception .

Let's consider Harris's campaign for the 2020 Democratic presidential nomination. Her initial launch was highly symbolic, drawing on her identity and personal story to energize voters. Her slogan, "For the People," evoked her background as a prosecutor and her commitment to justice. Yet, as the campaign progressed, her messaging became less clear, and voters began to scrutinize her record more closely. The initial excitement gave way to questions about her consistency on key issues like healthcare and criminal justice reform .

Harris's attempt to challenge Joe Biden on his past opposition to federally mandated busing during a primary debate is a prime example of the tension between symbolism and substance. The move was intended to highlight her commitment to civil rights and to draw a clear distinction between her and Biden. However, it backfired, as many voters perceived it as a politically motivated attack rather than a genuine critique. This incident underscored the limitations of relying too heavily on symbolic gestures without a consistent and clear policy agenda .

The gap between Harris's rhetoric and her actions has been a recurring theme throughout her career. As California Attorney General, she championed progressive causes like criminal justice reform and transparency in law enforcement. However, her office's record on police misconduct and her stance on the death penalty revealed a more complex reality. These inconsistencies have fueled critiques that Harris uses progressive rhetoric as a tool to appeal to voters without fully committing to the principles she espouses .

As Vice President, Harris continues to walk the tightrope between symbolism and substance. Her role is inherently symbolic, representing a break from the past and a step towards a more inclusive future. Yet, the expectations placed on her are immense, and the scrutiny is relentless. Her handling of issues like immigration, voting rights, and the COVID-19 response has been closely watched, with critics from both sides questioning her effectiveness and commitment to progressive ideals .

One of the most significant challenges Harris faces is the perception of voter deception. When politicians rely heavily on symbolic representation, they risk creating a disconnect between voters' expectations and the reality of their actions. This disconnect can lead to disillusionment and cynicism among voters, who feel betrayed when

the symbolic gestures do not translate into substantive policy changes
.

The use of identity politics to appeal to voters is a double-edged sword. On one hand, it can mobilize and energize voters, particularly those who have historically been marginalized. On the other hand, it can create unrealistic expectations and foster a sense of betrayal when the symbolic representation is not matched by tangible results. Harris's career illustrates this dynamic vividly, as she navigates the complex interplay between her identity and her policy record .

In conclusion, Kamala Harris's political journey is a testament to the power and pitfalls of symbolism in politics. Her identity as a Black and South Asian woman has been a powerful tool in her ascent to the vice presidency, inspiring countless voters and breaking barriers. However, the emphasis on symbolism has also exposed the risks of voter deception, where the focus on representation can overshadow critical examination of policy and performance.

As we continue to explore the intricacies of Harris's career, it's essential to critically assess the balance between substance and symbolism. Representation matters, but it must be coupled with genuine accountability and policy action to meet the expectations of voters.

Join us next in Chapter 13: Public Perception: Icon or Incompetent?, where we delve into the broader public perception of Kamala Harris and how it shapes her political trajectory.

Chapter 12
Public Perception
Icon or Incompetent?

Public perception is a powerful force in politics. It can make or break a career, shape narratives, and ultimately determine the success or failure of a politician. Kamala Harris, with her historic rise and complex political journey, has been both celebrated as an icon and criticized as incompetent. In this chapter, we dissect how public perception has shaped Harris's political trajectory and what it reveals about her leadership and the broader landscape of American politics.

Kamala Harris's public image has been a rollercoaster of highs and lows. From her celebrated entry into the national spotlight to the relentless scrutiny she faces as Vice President, Harris's journey offers a fascinating study in the power of perception.

When Harris first emerged on the national stage, she was hailed as a trailblazer. As the first Black and South Asian woman elected to the U.S. Senate from California, she quickly gained a reputation for her sharp questioning during Senate hearings and her advocacy for progressive causes. Her powerful presence during the Brett Kavanaugh and Jeff Sessions hearings, where she grilled the nominees with pointed questions, earned her national acclaim and established her as a rising star within the Democratic Party .

Her run for the 2020 Democratic presidential nomination further highlighted her ability to capture public attention. Harris's campaign launch in Oakland drew a massive crowd, and her speech resonated with themes of justice and equality. For many, she symbolized the future of the Democratic Party – a candidate who could unite diverse coalitions and push forward a progressive agenda.

However, the primary campaign also exposed the vulnerabilities in Harris's public image. Despite her strong start, Harris's campaign struggled with messaging and internal conflicts. Her inconsistent positions on key issues, such as healthcare, and her perceived attacks on Joe Biden during the debates led to a decline in support. By the time she suspended her campaign, public perception had shifted from seeing her as a frontrunner to viewing her campaign as faltering and unorganized .

As Vice President, Harris's public perception continues to be a mixed bag. Her historic achievement of becoming the first woman, first Black woman, and first South Asian woman to hold the office is a significant milestone that has inspired millions. Her presence in the White House is a powerful symbol of progress and representation.

Yet, the challenges of the vice presidency have also exposed Harris to intense scrutiny. Her handling of the immigration crisis at the southern border has been a focal point of criticism. Both progressives and conservatives have taken issue with her approach – progressives argue that she has not done enough to address the humanitarian aspects of the crisis, while conservatives criticize her for perceived leniency. The mixed responses highlight the difficulty of navigating such a complex and polarizing issue .

Harris's role in advocating for voting rights has also been a critical aspect of her vice presidency. Her passionate speeches and calls for federal legislation to protect voting access have resonated with many. However, the lack of substantial legislative victories in this area has led to frustration among her supporters. The perception of Harris as a powerful advocate is tempered by the reality of the political gridlock she faces .

Media portrayal plays a significant role in shaping public perception of Harris. Major news outlets have often framed her tenure through the lens of her identity and the historic nature of her role. This focus on her identity has been both a source of strength and a point of contention. While it underscores the significance of her achievements, it can also detract from substantive discussions about her policy positions and leadership capabilities .

Social media further amplifies the polarized views of Harris. Supporters celebrate her achievements and defend her against attacks, while detractors criticize her performance and question her competence. The echo chambers of social media often reinforce existing biases, making it challenging to find balanced and nuanced perspectives .

· · ·

Harris's public perception is also shaped by her interactions with the media and the public. Her communication style – characterized by a combination of warmth, assertiveness, and sometimes cautiousness – has been both praised and criticized. Her ability to connect with diverse audiences and articulate her vision is a significant asset, but moments of perceived evasiveness or lack of clarity have fueled criticism .

In conclusion, Kamala Harris's public perception is a complex interplay of symbolism, media portrayal, and her actual performance. She is celebrated as an icon and a symbol of progress, yet also criticized for perceived inconsistencies and policy shortcomings. This duality reflects the broader challenges faced by politicians who navigate the treacherous waters of public opinion.

As we continue to explore the intricacies of Harris's political career, it's crucial to understand how these perceptions impact her ability to lead and implement her agenda. The next chapter will take us beyond American borders to examine Harris's global presence and the international implications of her role.

Join us next in Chapter 14: Global Embarrassment: Harris on the World Stage, where we delve into her international influence and the challenges she faces in the global arena.

Chapter 13
Global Embarrassment
Harris on the World Stage

Welcome to the international arena, where the stakes are high, and the scrutiny is relentless. Kamala Harris, as the Vice President of the United States, plays a critical role on the global stage. But how has she fared in this complex and unforgiving environment? This chapter examines Harris's international influence, the challenges she faces, and the perceptions of her performance beyond American borders. Buckle up – it's time to see how Harris handles the pressure of global leadership.

Kamala Harris's rise to the vice presidency marked a historic moment not just for the United States, but for the world. As the first woman of color to hold the office, her presence in international forums carries significant symbolic weight. However, symbolism alone is not enough to navigate the intricacies of global politics. Harris's effectiveness on the world stage is a mix of notable achievements and significant criticisms.

. . .

One of Harris's earliest and most high-profile international assignments was addressing the root causes of migration from Central America. President Biden tasked her with leading diplomatic efforts to curb the influx of migrants at the U.S. southern border by improving conditions in countries like Guatemala, Honduras, and El Salvador. Harris's approach focused on tackling corruption, enhancing economic opportunities, and improving security in the region .

During her first international trip as Vice President to Guatemala and Mexico, Harris emphasized the need for cooperation and long-term solutions. Her message was clear: addressing the root causes of migration would require significant investment and collaboration. However, her trip was not without controversy. Her blunt statement, "Do not come," directed at potential migrants, drew criticism from both sides of the political spectrum. Progressives argued that it contradicted the administration's commitment to humane immigration policies, while conservatives questioned its effectiveness .

Harris's handling of the migration issue illustrates the broader challenges she faces on the international stage. Balancing domestic political pressures with the complex realities of international diplomacy is no easy task. Her efforts to engage with Central American leaders and address systemic issues are commendable, but the tangible results have been slow to materialize.

In addition to her work on immigration, Harris has been involved in various international efforts related to climate change, cybersecurity, and economic cooperation. Her participation in global forums, such as the Munich Security Conference and meetings with international leaders, highlights her role in shaping U.S. foreign policy. However, her relative lack of foreign policy experience compared to her predecessors has been a point of criticism .

One of the most scrutinized aspects of Harris's international presence is her communication style and diplomatic acumen. Critics argue that her interactions with foreign leaders have sometimes lacked the nuance and gravitas expected of a high-ranking official. Her responses to questions about international issues have occasionally been seen as evasive or overly scripted, fueling perceptions of inadequacy .

The media's portrayal of Harris's international engagements has also influenced public perception. Major news outlets have often focused on her symbolic significance rather than her policy achievements, reinforcing the narrative of Harris as a groundbreaking figure but not necessarily an effective diplomat. This focus on symbolism can obscure critical evaluations of her performance and policy impact .

Harris's challenges on the world stage are compounded by the broader geopolitical context. The Biden administration's efforts to restore alliances and rebuild America's global standing after the Trump era require careful and strategic diplomacy. Harris's role in this effort is crucial, but the road is fraught with obstacles, including managing relations with adversaries like China and Russia, addressing global health crises, and navigating economic uncertainties .

Despite these challenges, Harris has also had moments of success and positive impact. Her advocacy for global health initiatives, support for climate action, and engagement in economic diplomacy have been well-received in many quarters. Her ability to bring attention to issues like gender equality and human rights on the international stage underscores the importance of having diverse voices in global leadership .

In conclusion, Kamala Harris's performance on the world stage is a study in contrasts. She represents a significant and symbolic break from the past, bringing a fresh perspective to international diplomacy. However, her relative inexperience and the immense challenges she faces have led to mixed reviews. Harris's success in the international arena will depend on her ability to translate symbolic representation into substantive policy achievements and to navigate the complex landscape of global politics with greater confidence and skill.

As we continue to unravel the multifaceted career of Kamala Harris, it's essential to understand the broader implications of her role. The next chapter will dive into the criticisms and controversies that have dogged her career, offering a comprehensive analysis of the key issues and their impact on her political trajectory.

Join us next in Chapter 15: The Critics Speak: Unpacking the Kamala Controversies, where we delve into the most significant critiques and controversies surrounding Harris and what they reveal about her leadership and character.

Chapter 14
The Critics Speak
Unpacking the Kamala Controversies

Brace yourself, because it's time to confront the critics and delve into the controversies that have shadowed Kamala Harris's career. From her time as a prosecutor to her role as Vice President, Harris has faced relentless scrutiny and fierce criticism. This chapter will dissect these controversies, examining their validity and impact on her political trajectory. We'll leave no stone unturned in our quest to understand the complex narrative that surrounds her.

Harris's Record as a Prosecutor

As San Francisco District Attorney and later as California Attorney General, Harris adopted policies often seen as tough on crime. This included aggressive prosecution of drug offenses and support for laws imposing harsh penalties, which critics argue disproportionately affected minority communities, contradicting her later progressive stances on criminal justice reform .

.   .   .

One of the most controversial policies during her tenure was prosecuting parents of truant children. While intended to address chronic absenteeism, it was criticized for criminalizing poverty and targeting low-income families. Harris later expressed regret over the unintended consequences, but the criticism remains significant .

Handling of Police Misconduct

Harris's tenure as Attorney General was marked by reluctance to support independent investigations into police shootings and misconduct. Despite public outcry and a growing national movement for police accountability, she maintained that local authorities should handle such investigations, leading to accusations of protecting law enforcement at the expense of justice .

Her defense of the death penalty, despite personal opposition, further fueled criticisms of inconsistency and political expediency .

Shifting Positions on Key Issues

Harris's stance on healthcare, particularly her support for "Medicare for All," evolved significantly during her 2020 presidential campaign. Initially a strong proponent, she later proposed a plan that included a role for private insurance, leading to accusations of flip-flopping and political calculation .

.   .   .

Handling of Immigration

As Vice President, Harris has been tasked with addressing the root causes of migration from Central America. Her blunt message to potential migrants – "Do not come" – drew backlash from both progressives and conservatives, highlighting the delicate balance she must strike in addressing complex issues .

Internal Management and Staff Turnover

Reports of high staff turnover and allegations of a toxic work environment have raised questions about Harris's management style and ability to maintain a cohesive and effective team. These issues have fueled narratives of instability and poor leadership .

Public Perception and Media Criticism

The media's portrayal of Harris has been a double-edged sword. While her historic achievements are celebrated, she is also subjected to intense scrutiny, often harsher than her male counterparts. This scrutiny includes critiques of her communication style, public appearances, and handling of press interactions. The media's focus on her identity sometimes overshadows substantive discussions about her policies and performance .

Public perception of Harris is deeply polarized. Supporters view her as a trailblazer and symbol of progress, while detractors criticize her as ineffective and overly ambitious. This polarization reflects broader societal divides and the challenging landscape of contemporary American politics .

Conclusion

The controversies surrounding Kamala Harris are a reflection of the complexities of her career and the broader challenges she faces in American politics. Her record is a mix of significant achievements and contentious decisions, illustrating the difficulties of navigating a political landscape fraught with contradictions and competing demands.

Understanding these controversies in context reveals not only the strengths and weaknesses of Harris as a leader but also the broader dynamics of American politics, where symbolism, substance, and public perception are in constant interplay.

Chapter 15
Future Nightmare
What Harris Means for America

Hold on tight, because we're about to gaze into the crystal ball and examine the potential future impacts of Kamala Harris's political career on America. As a trailblazer and a highly scrutinized figure, Harris's trajectory holds significant implications for the country's political landscape. Will her influence usher in an era of progress and inclusivity, or will it exacerbate existing divisions and challenges? This chapter delves into the possible futures shaped by Harris's role in American politics.

Kamala Harris stands at a pivotal crossroads in American history. Her rise to the vice presidency symbolizes a break from the past and the promise of a more diverse and inclusive political future. However, the path ahead is fraught with complexities and potential pitfalls. Here, we explore the possible scenarios and their implications for the nation.

. . .

Imagine a future where Kamala Harris emerges as a champion for progressive reforms. Her relentless advocacy for social justice could drive significant advancements in areas like criminal justice reform, healthcare, and economic equality. Harris could leverage her position to push for bold legislation that addresses systemic inequalities, fostering a fairer and more just society. Her policies could empower marginalized communities, inspiring greater political engagement and representation, and fostering a more inclusive democracy.

However, navigating the deeply polarized political environment presents a formidable challenge. Harris's efforts to enact her agenda could be stymied by the relentless partisan gridlock that defines contemporary American politics. The struggle to find common ground with Republicans might stall critical legislative initiatives, leading to frustration and disillusionment among her supporters. In response, Harris may be forced to make strategic compromises. While this pragmatic approach might yield some legislative victories, it could also dilute the boldness of her progressive vision, leading to criticisms from the left .

Looking towards future elections, Harris's success or failure as Vice President will likely influence the political landscape. A successful tenure could set a powerful precedent, paving the way for more women and people of color to seek and attain high office, transforming the political scene. Conversely, perceived failures could reinforce existing biases and hinder progress towards greater diversity in leadership. Harris's potential bid for the presidency in 2024 is a topic of considerable speculation. Her candidacy would undoubtedly energize segments of the Democratic base, but it could also face significant resistance from both within and outside the party. Her ability to unite a broad coalition will be crucial to her success .

· · ·

On the economic front, Harris's policies, if successfully implemented, could have lasting impacts on the American economy. Initiatives aimed at reducing income inequality, expanding healthcare access, and investing in education and infrastructure could foster long-term economic growth and stability. Imagine a future where Harris's focus on addressing economic disparities leads to targeted interventions that uplift disadvantaged communities, creating a more equitable society. However, the feasibility of these reforms in a contentious political climate remains uncertain, and the road to economic justice is fraught with obstacles .

Globally, Harris's role in foreign policy could help restore and strengthen international alliances that were strained during the previous administration. Her diplomatic efforts could enhance America's standing on the global stage and promote collaborative approaches to global challenges. Imagine Harris playing a crucial role in managing global crises like climate change and international conflicts, shaping America's role as a global leader. However, her relative lack of foreign policy experience compared to her predecessors has been a point of criticism, and her ability to effectively manage these crises will be a critical test of her leadership .

Yet, the potential for political backlash is ever-present. Harris's progressive agenda and identity politics could provoke a significant reaction from conservative and moderate voters. This reactionary response could manifest in various forms, from increased political polarization to the rise of more extreme candidates and movements. The cultural and political divisions that Harris's leadership may exacerbate could lead to intensified cultural wars, influencing public discourse and policy-making .

. . .

In conclusion, Kamala Harris's future impact on America is a tapestry of potential outcomes, each woven with opportunities and challenges. Her ability to navigate the complexities of American politics, push forward progressive reforms, and unite a diverse electorate will determine her legacy. As the nation grapples with profound changes and uncertainties, Harris's role will be pivotal in shaping the future trajectory of American democracy.

The journey of Kamala Harris is far from over, and the stakes are higher than ever. As we move towards the final chapter, we reflect on the lessons learned and the path forward.

Conclusion
Escaping the Identity Politics Quagmire

As we draw to a close, it's time to reflect on the journey we've taken through the complex landscape of Kamala Harris's political career. We've explored her triumphs and failures, her symbolic significance, and the substantive impact of her policies. But perhaps the most pressing question remains: How can America move beyond the traps of identity politics to achieve genuine progress?

Kamala Harris's rise to power is a testament to the power of representation. Her identity as a Black and South Asian woman has broken barriers and inspired millions. However, the pitfalls of identity politics have also become apparent. While representation is vital, it must be coupled with substantive policy actions to create real change.

Throughout Harris's career, we've seen the delicate balance she has tried to maintain between her progressive ideals and the pragmatic realities of governance. This balancing act highlights a broader issue in American politics – the tension between symbolic representation and substantive action. Identity politics can sometimes obscure critical policy discussions, reducing complex individuals to mere symbols rather than focusing on their capabilities and policies.

The Dangers of Over-reliance on Identity Politics

Kamala Harris's political narrative is deeply intertwined with her identity. While this has garnered significant support, it has also led to criticisms that she relies too heavily on her identity to deflect from policy shortcomings and controversies. For instance, her record as a prosecutor has come under scrutiny for policies that disproportionately affected minority communities. Despite her progressive rhetoric, her actions often reflected a more conservative approach, leading to accusations of political opportunism .

The Need for Substance Over Symbolism

To move beyond the identity politics quagmire, America needs a more nuanced approach to representation. This involves celebrating diversity while also demanding accountability and tangible results from our leaders. Representation should not be an end in itself but a means to achieving greater equity and justice.

Harris's career offers valuable lessons in this regard. Her journey underscores the importance of scrutinizing the policies and actions of our leaders, regardless of their identity. It also highlights the need for a more inclusive political discourse that goes beyond surface-level representation to address the systemic issues that affect marginalized communities .

Fostering an Informed and Engaged Electorate

One way to achieve this is through fostering a more informed and engaged electorate. Voters must be encouraged to look beyond identity markers and evaluate candidates based on their policy positions, track records, and ability to effect change. This requires a concerted effort from the media, educational institutions, and civil society to promote critical thinking and civic engagement .

Moreover, political leaders must be willing to take bold and principled stands on key issues. While strategic compromises are sometimes necessary, leaders should not shy away from advocating for transformative policies that address the root causes of inequality and injustice. This requires courage, resilience, and a genuine commitment to serving the public good.

The Implications of Harris's Potential Presidency

Kamala Harris's role as Vice President and her potential future political ambitions will continue to shape the conversation around identity politics in America. Her ability to navigate these challenges and deliver on her promises will be a critical test of her leadership. As she works to implement her agenda, she must strive to bridge the gap between symbolic representation and substantive action.

. . .

However, Harris's history of political missteps, from her ineffective handling of her presidential campaign to her contentious tenure as Vice President, suggests she may not possess the qualities needed to effectively lead the nation. Her inability to maintain consistent policy positions, coupled with her reliance on identity politics, raises serious doubts about her suitability for the presidency .

A Path Forward for American Politics

In the broader context, America's journey towards a more just and equitable society depends on its ability to move beyond the limitations of identity politics. This means embracing the diversity of experiences and perspectives that make up the nation while also holding our leaders accountable for their actions. It means valuing representation, not as an end, but as a catalyst for real change.

As we reflect on Kamala Harris's career, we see a leader who embodies both the promise and the pitfalls of identity politics. Her story is a mirror reflecting the broader dynamics of American society – the struggles, the triumphs, and the ongoing quest for justice. By learning from her journey, we can chart a path forward that transcends the limitations of identity politics and builds a more inclusive and equitable future.

Thank you for joining us on this exploration of Kamala Harris's political career and the broader implications of identity politics. The journey doesn't end here. The lessons we've uncovered are just the beginning of a broader conversation about the future of American democracy. Together, we can work towards a society where representation and substance go hand in hand, creating a more just and equitable world for all.

Disclaimer and Encouragement for Independent Research

As readers of "Beyond Identity Politics - The BIGGEST Mistake America Will Make: The Truth About Kamala Harris," we encourage you to conduct your own research and verify the information presented in this book. The complexities and nuances of political careers, especially those of high-profile figures like Kamala Harris, require thorough examination from multiple perspectives.

We have made every effort to ensure the accuracy of the content based on available data and sources at the time of writing. However, the dynamic nature of politics means that new information and interpretations can emerge. We urge you to consult a variety of sources, check factual claims, and engage in critical thinking as you form your own opinions.

Thank you for taking the time to read this book. Your commitment to seeking the truth and understanding the broader implications of political actions and policies is crucial for a vibrant and informed democracy.

www.ingramcontent.com/pod-product-compliance
Lightning Source LLC
Chambersburg PA
CBHW050830250726
48653CB00006B/2529